Crafts for
Kwanzaa

Light the Kwanzaa Candles....

Crafts for Kwanzaa

by Kathy Ross
Illustrated by Sharon Lane Holm

SCHOLASTIC INC.
New York Toronto London Auckland Sydney

For Greyson and Allison

ISBN 0-590-67719-5

12 11 10 9 8 7 6 5 4 3 2 1   5 6 7 8 9/9 0/0

Printed in the U.S.A.   09

First Scholastic printing, September 1995

Contents

Celebrating Kwanzaa

Kwanzaa is a holiday celebrating the African roots of black Americans. It begins on December 26 and lasts for seven days. It celebrates the shared life and history of black people, both past and present. The colors of Kwanzaa are red, black, and green—the colors of the flag created by the African-American leader Marcus Garvey at the beginning of the twentieth century. Red represents the struggle of black people for freedom. Black is for black people united. And green symbolizes the future of black people.

The African language of Swahili is used to name the symbols and words used at Kwanzaa time. The name "Kwanzaa" itself comes from a Swahili word for the first fruits of the harvest. The values expressed through this holiday are reflected in the **nguzo saba** (or seven principles) of Kwanzaa written by Dr. Maulana Karenga, a teacher who created this celebration in 1966.

Nguzo Saba
The Seven Principles of Kwanzaa

Umoja (Unity)
Kujichagulia (Self-Determination)
Ujima (Collective Work and Responsibility)
Ujamaa (Cooperative Economics)
Nia (Purpose)
Kuumba (Creativity)
Imani (Faith)

Paper Mat

The **mkeka** is a mat on which the symbols of Kwanzaa are placed. It represents the importance of history and tradition within the black American family. Make a mat for your Kwanzaa celebration.

Here is what you need:

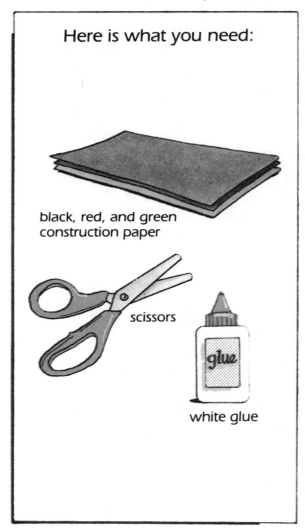

black, red, and green construction paper

scissors

white glue

Here is what you do:

 1. Fold the black construction paper in half lengthwise and cut strips about 1 inch (2.5 centimeters) apart across the paper from the fold to about 1 inch from the edge. Do not cut the paper apart.

2. Cut inch-wide strips from red and green paper and weave them in alternating colors through the black paper. Glue the ends of the strips to hold them in place.

If you would like your mat to last a long time, cover it on both sides with clear contact paper.

Foil Cup

Everyone drinks from the **kikombe cha umoja**, or big cup, at Kwanzaa time. The cup represents the value of the black family and community living and working together.

Here is what you need:

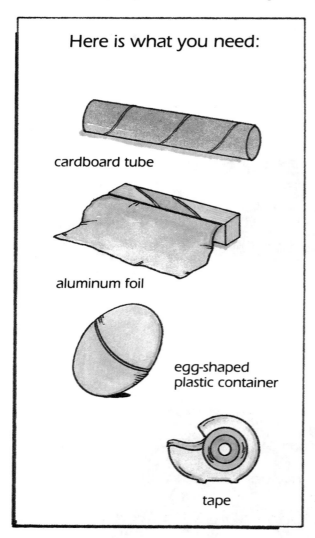

cardboard tube

aluminum foil

egg-shaped plastic container

tape

Here is what you do:

1. Cut a 2-inch (5-centimeter) piece from the cardboard tube to use as the stem of your cup.

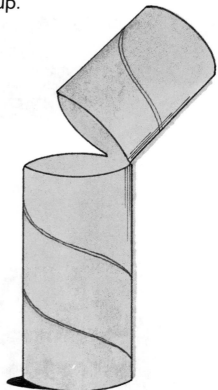

Tape the tube to the top of the small part of the plastic egg to form the base of your cup. Tape the large part of the egg to the top of the tube to form a cup.

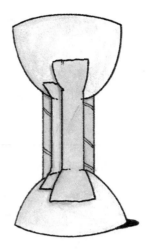

2. Cover the entire cup with foil so that it looks like it's made of metal.

Harvest Banner

Mazao, the fruits and vegetables, represent the fruit of all work. Make a harvest banner of fruits and vegetables.

Here is what you need:

light-colored paper or fabric

stick to hang the banner on

yarn

different fruits and vegetables to print with

white glue

poster paint in the colors of the produce you have chosen

paintbrush

Here is what you do:

1. Most fruits and vegetables will need to be cut in half so that you can use the flat inside part to print a picture of the fruit on your fabric or paper. Apples, oranges, pears, carrots, and green peppers all print especially well, but you will need to ask an adult to help you cut them. Corn prints well from the outside.

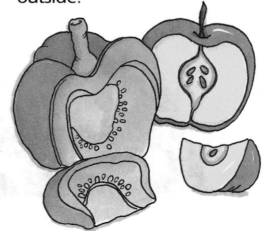

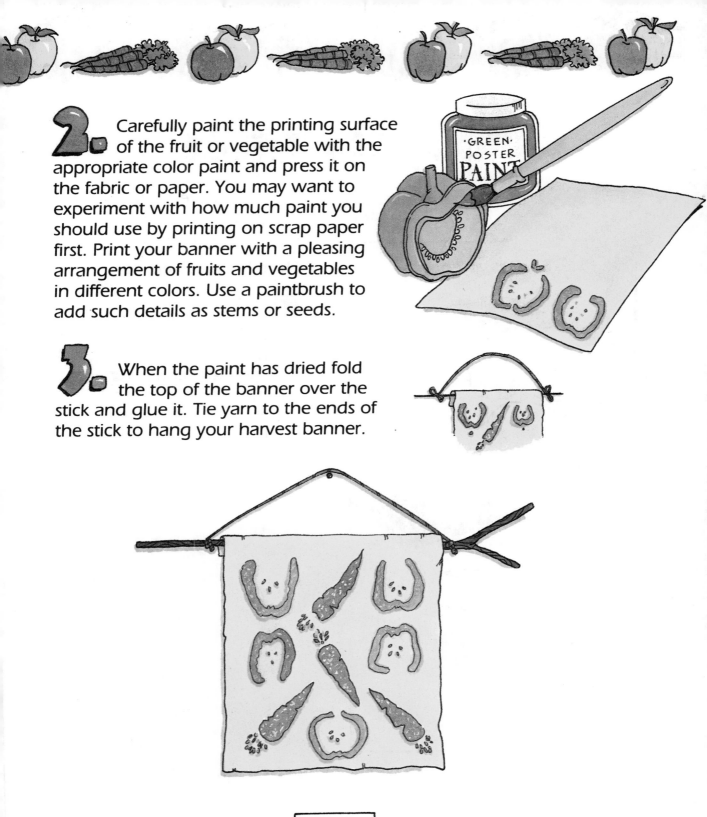

2. Carefully paint the printing surface of the fruit or vegetable with the appropriate color paint and press it on the fabric or paper. You may want to experiment with how much paint you should use by printing on scrap paper first. Print your banner with a pleasing arrangement of fruits and vegetables in different colors. Use a paintbrush to add such details as stems or seeds.

3. When the paint has dried fold the top of the banner over the stick and glue it. Tie yarn to the ends of the stick to hang your harvest banner.

Pumpkin Trivet

Here is what you need:

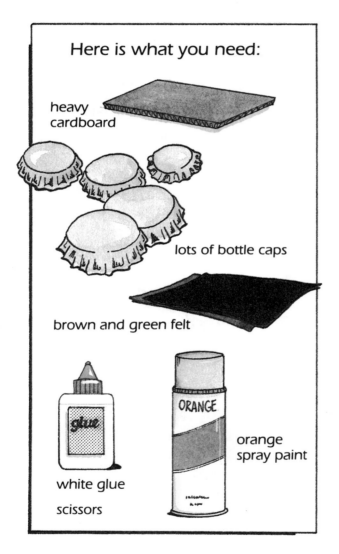

heavy cardboard

lots of bottle caps

brown and green felt

white glue

scissors

ORANGE

orange spray paint

Here is what you do:

1. Sketch a round pumpkin shape on the cardboard about 8 inches (20 centimeters) around. Add a stem and leaf outline to the top. Cut the pumpkin out of the cardboard.

Cover the round pumpkin (not the leaf and stem) with glue. Cover the glued pumpkin with bottle caps with the metal side up.

2. When the glue has dried completely take the trivet outside and spray paint it with orange spray paint. (Ask an adult to help you with this.) Cover the stem with brown felt and the leaf with green felt.

You can use any fruit or vegetable shape you want to make a trivet. Just draw the shape of the vegetable or fruit you choose and spray paint it in the appropriate color. Trivets make very nice Kwanzaa gifts.

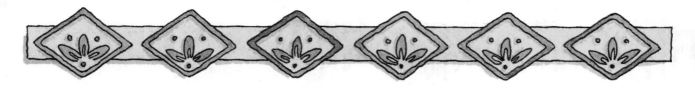

Corn Necklace

Munhindi means corn. The corn represents the children of a family. Make your mom a necklace with one ear of corn for each child in your family.

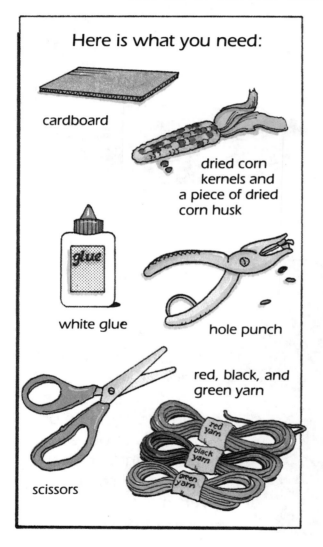

Here is what you need:

cardboard

dried corn kernels and a piece of dried corn husk

white glue

hole punch

red, black, and green yarn

scissors

Here is what you do:

1. Cut a corn shape from cardboard for each ear of corn on your necklace. Punch two holes in the top of each one and string them across strands of the three colors of yarn cut to form a necklace.

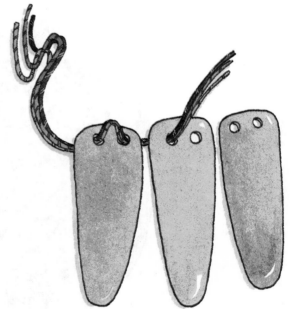

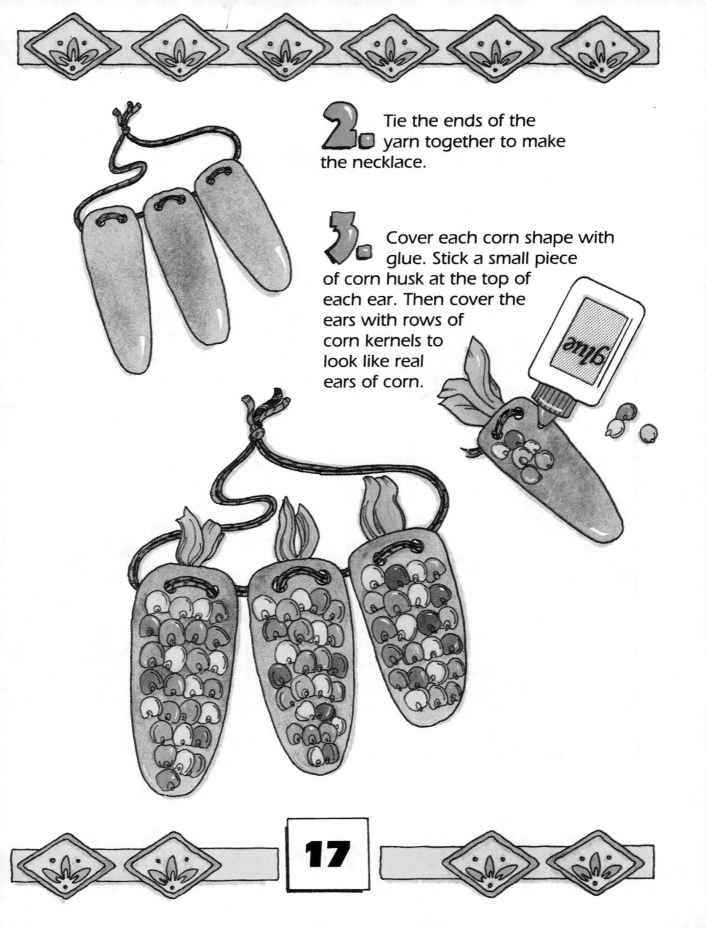

2. Tie the ends of the yarn together to make the necklace.

3. Cover each corn shape with glue. Stick a small piece of corn husk at the top of each ear. Then cover the ears with rows of corn kernels to look like real ears of corn.

glue

Tissue Paper Corn

Here is what you need:

brown, tan, orange, and yellow tissue paper

white glue

scissors

plastic wrap

tape

Here is what you do:

1. Cut some of each color tissue into 1-inch (2.5-centimeter) squares. Draw a full-size outline of an ear of corn on a square of plastic wrap and fill the outline in completely with a thin layer of glue.

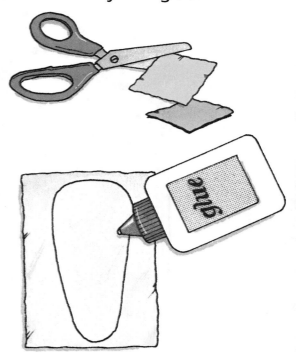

Arrange the squares of tissue on the glue in a corn shape. Make at least two ears of corn.

2. When the glue has dried completely, peel each ear off the plastic and trim it into the shape of an ear of corn. The glue will make the tissue shiny on one side. This will be the front of the corn.

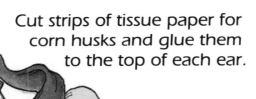

Cut strips of tissue paper for corn husks and glue them to the top of each ear.

Tape your corn to a sunny window so the light can shine through the colored tissue kernels.

Kwanzaa Candles Card

The candleholder is called the **kinara,** and the seven candles are called the **mishumaa saba**. There is one black candle in the center, with three red candles on the left and three green candles on the right. The black candle is lit on the first day of Kwanzaa and another candle is added each day until all seven are lighted.

Here is what you need:

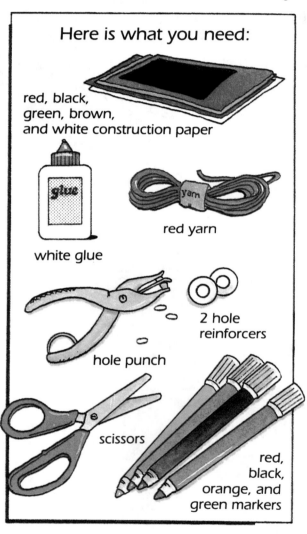

red, black, green, brown, and white construction paper

white glue

red yarn

hole punch

2 hole reinforcers

scissors

red, black, orange, and green markers

Here is what you do:

1. Fold a piece of white construction paper in half. Glue a strip of brown construction paper across the bottom (open) end for the candleholder. Cut three red candles, one black candle, and three green candles and glue them across the candleholder, slipping the bottoms of the candles under the brown paper. Cut a flame shape out of the paper at the top of each candle. Glue the bottom edges of the card together.

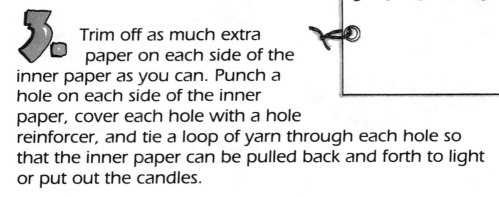

2. Cut a piece of white construction paper to exactly fit inside the card. Slide it in and use an orange marker to color in the candle flame holes at the top of each candle. When you move the paper to one side the flames should be hidden between the candles as though they were not lit.

3. Trim off as much extra paper on each side of the inner paper as you can. Punch a hole on each side of the inner paper, cover each hole with a hole reinforcer, and tie a loop of yarn through each hole so that the inner paper can be pulled back and forth to light or put out the candles.

Write "Light the Kwanzaa Candles" across the top of your card and your Kwanzaa greeting on the back.

Kwanzaa
Candle Favors

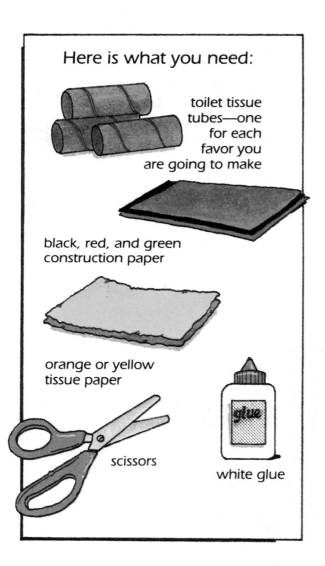

Here is what you need:

toilet tissue tubes—one for each favor you are going to make

black, red, and green construction paper

orange or yellow tissue paper

scissors

white glue

Here is what you do:

1. To make each candle favor cover a cardboard tube with glue and then black, green, or red construction paper.

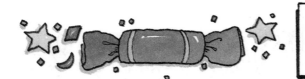

2. Cut a 10-inch (25-centimeter) square of tissue paper and place candy, nuts, or a small prize in the middle of the square. Gather the tissue paper up around the prize and push the prize down into the tube candle so that the ends of the tissue paper are sticking out like a candle flame.

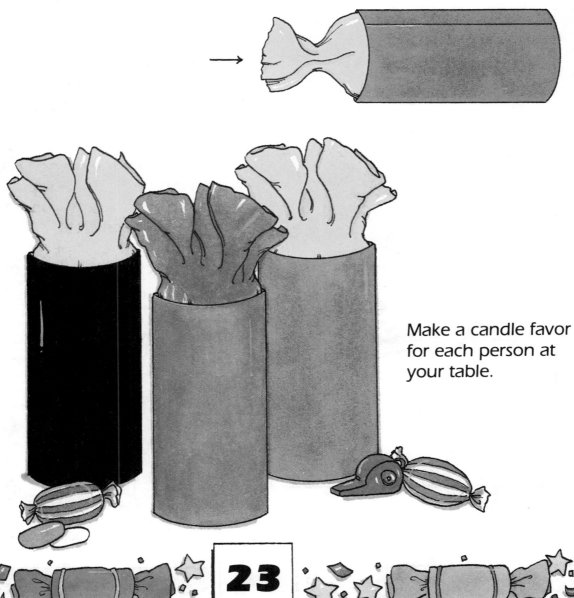

Make a candle favor for each person at your table.

Kwanzaa Candles Game

Here is what you need:

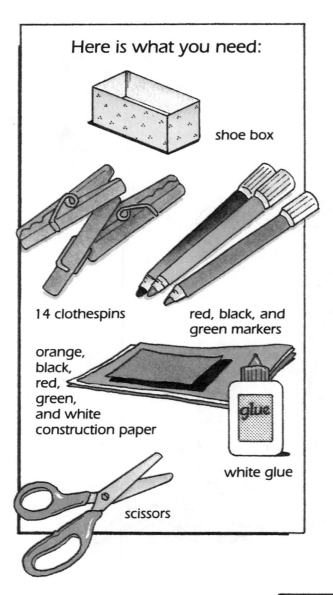

shoe box

14 clothespins

red, black, and green markers

orange, black, red, green, and white construction paper

white glue

scissors

Here is what you do:

1. You will need to make six red, six green, and two black candles from construction paper. Make them the height and width of the clothespins. Cut out 14 flame shapes from the orange paper and glue one to the top of each candle. Then glue one candle to each clothespin so that it can be clamped on the shoe box with the flame on top.

2. Cut 14 cards about 2 inches (5 centimeters) square from the white paper. Draw a black candle on two cards, a red candle on six cards, and a green candle on six cards.

Here is how to play the game:

This game is for two players. Give each player one black, three red, and three green candles. Put the cards face down in the shoe box. The players sit facing each other with the box between them. The object of the game is to see who can get all of their Kwanzaa candles lined up on the box first. The candles must be placed in the order they are lighted for each day of Kwanzaa. The black candle comes first (in the middle), then the red candles on the left, then the green candles on the right. Players alternate red and green until all seven candles are on the box. To get candles, players take turns drawing from

the cards in the box. If the player uses a card he or she takes it from the box, but if the card cannot be used, it is mixed back into the pile. Players may draw cards to see who goes first, with black being first.

Corn Print
Wrapping Paper

Zawadi means gifts. The last day of Kwanzaa
is a time for sharing gifts. Here are some ideas for
wrapping and tagging your gifts.

Here is what you need:

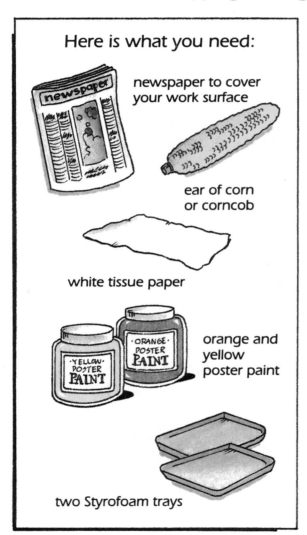

newspaper to cover
your work surface

ear of corn
or corncob

white tissue paper

orange and
yellow
poster paint

two Styrofoam trays

Here is what you do:

1. Pour one color
of paint
into each tray.

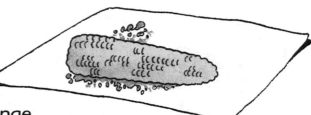 **2.** Roll the corn in the yellow paint first. Then roll it across the paper in several different directions to print the paper with the design of the corn.

3. Do the same with the orange paint. Let the tissue dry flat.

Dyed Wrapping Paper

Here is what you need:

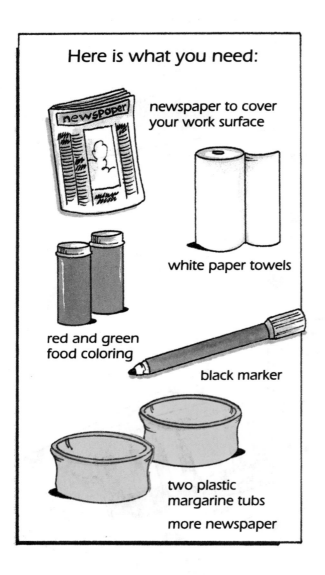

newspaper to cover your work surface

white paper towels

red and green food coloring

black marker

two plastic margarine tubs

more newspaper

Here is what you do:

1. Put about 1/2 inch (1 centimeter) of water in each margarine tub. Add about 1/2 teaspoon of red food coloring to one tub and 1/2 teaspoon of green food coloring to the other tub.

2. Fold a paper towel square all the way across like a fan, folding first in one direction and then in the other. Now fold the long folded strip like a fan, so that you end up with a folded square of paper. Dip the two opposite corners in one color and the remaining two corners in the other color. Blot the colored towel between more paper towels to squeeze out the extra water.

3. Open the paper carefully and let it dry flat on newspaper. Then use a black marker to outline the patches of color.

Candle Gift Tag

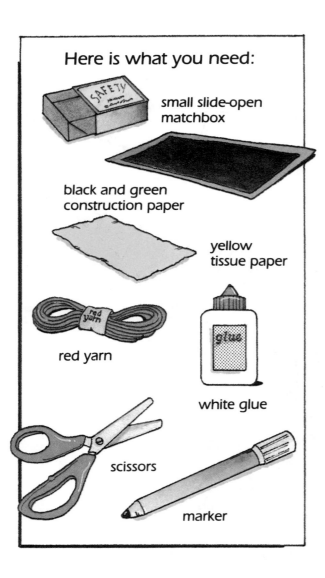

Here is what you need:

small slide-open matchbox

black and green construction paper

yellow tissue paper

red yarn

white glue

scissors

marker

Here is what you do:

1. Cover the outside of the box with black paper. Slide the box open and glue some yellow tissue paper inside so that when the box is open it will look like the flame at the top of a black candle.

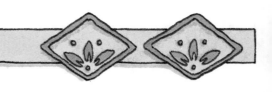

2. Poke a hole in the top of the inner box just above the flame. Tie a loop of red yarn through the hole so that you can pull the flame up.

3. Cut a small piece of green paper to glue on the front of the candle. Write "Happy Kwanzaa" and the name of the person you are giving the gift to. At the bottom of the tag write "pull to light candle." Close the box so that the flame is hidden inside and attach it to a gift.

HAPPY
KWANZAA
TO
MIKE

pull to light
candle

Kwanzaa Memory Book

Make a memory book for photographs and drawings of your Kwanzaa celebration. This book would make a nice Kwanzaa gift.

Here is what you need:

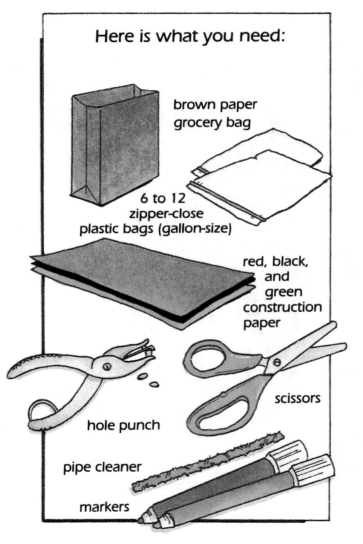

brown paper grocery bag

6 to 12 zipper-close plastic bags (gallon-size)

red, black, and green construction paper

scissors

hole punch

pipe cleaner

markers

Here is what you do:

1. The plastic bags will be the pages of your book. Stack them so that the bottoms of the bags are on your left. From the brown paper bag, cut a cover that folds around the plastic bags to form both the front and back of the book. (The cover should be a little larger than the pages.) Make sure all the pages are lined up inside the cover.

Then punch a hole near the top and the bottom of the fold. Use pieces of pipe cleaner strung through the holes, with the ends twisted together, to hold the book together.

2. Use markers to color a picture on the front of your memory book. Cut pieces of red, green, or black construction paper to fit inside each of the plastic pages of your book. Then you can tape photographs, drawings, and other small memories of your holiday celebration to the front and back of each construction paper sheet, and they will be protected by the plastic pages.

My Kwanzaa Memory Book

Paper Flag

The **bendera**, or flag, is black, red, and green—the colors of Kwanzaa. Here are some ideas for making your own flags.

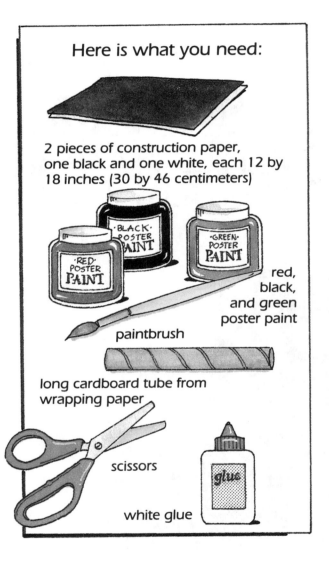

Here is what you need:

2 pieces of construction paper, one black and one white, each 12 by 18 inches (30 by 46 centimeters)

red, black, and green poster paint

paintbrush

long cardboard tube from wrapping paper

scissors

white glue

Here is what you do:

Paint a band of black across the middle third of the white paper. Paint the top third red and the bottom third green.

2. Cut the black construction paper to fit around the cardboard tube to cover it, and glue it in place.

Glue your flag to one end of the tube, making sure that the red stripe is on the top.

Flag Favors

Kwanzaa celebrations include a feast, or **karamu**, on December 31. You can make a flag for each person at your feast.

Here is what you need:

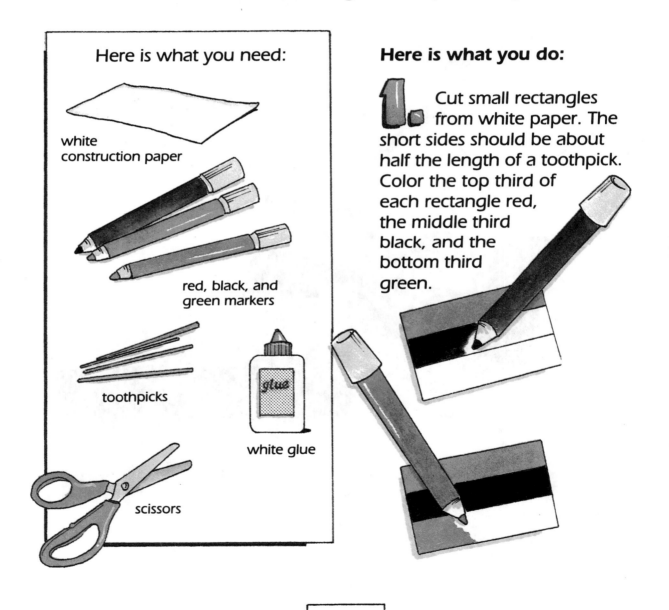

white construction paper

red, black, and green markers

toothpicks

white glue

scissors

Here is what you do:

1. Cut small rectangles from white paper. The short sides should be about half the length of a toothpick. Color the top third of each rectangle red, the middle third black, and the bottom third green.

2. Glue each flag to a toothpick pole. Stick the toothpick in a cupcake, roll, or piece of fruit to make the flag stand.

Flag Pin

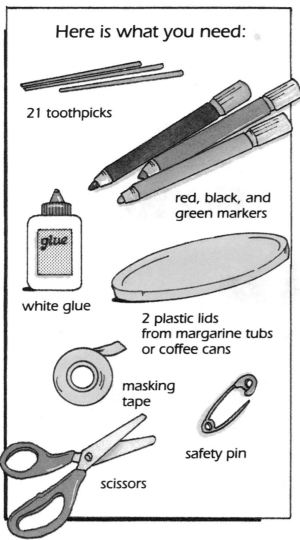

Here is what you need:

21 toothpicks

red, black, and green markers

glue

white glue

2 plastic lids from margarine tubs or coffee cans

masking tape

safety pin

scissors

Here is what you do:

1. Use markers to color seven toothpicks red, seven black, and seven green.

2. Place the seven red toothpicks on one plastic lid to form a red band. Next put the seven black ones, and then the seven green ones. Squeeze white glue all over the square shape formed by the toothpicks. Press the second plastic lid over the glue-covered toothpicks and turn the flag onto the second lid so that the glue is between the plastic and the toothpicks. Remove the first lid. Turning the flag onto the second lid will help it to hold its shape while it dries. Make sure all the toothpicks are even with each other. Then let the glue dry completely.

3. When the flag is dry, peel it off the lid and trim the toothpick points from both sides with a pair of scissors.

4. Glue a safety pin to the back of the flag. Use masking tape to hold the safety pin in place while the glue dries.

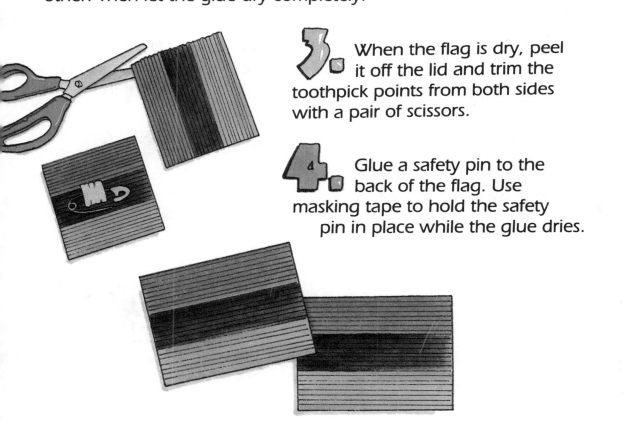

Harvest Frame

At Kwanzaa time many people hang the **nguzo saba**,
the seven principles of Kwanzaa, on the wall.

Here is what you need:

empty cereal box

green
construction paper

magazine or supermarket
flyer pictures of fruits
and vegetables

red yarn

white glue

scissors

stapler

Here is what you do:

1. Open both ends of the cereal box and cut the back off. Trim the four flaps that remain around the box front to equal widths. Cut a sheet of green paper to fit over the colored picture on the cereal box front and glue it in place.

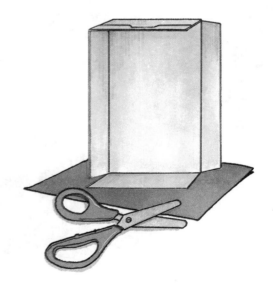

2. Fold the four flaps in over the green paper to form a frame and glue them in place.

3. Glue on pictures of fruits and vegetables to cover the frame. Staple a yarn hanger to the top of the frame.

4. Write the **nguzo saba** inside the frame, or glue in a photograph or drawing of your Kwanzaa celebration.

NGUZO SABA
Umoja
Kujichagulia
Ujima
Ujamaa
Nia
Kuumba
Imani

made by –
Mike

Kwanzaa Hug Card

Here is what you need:

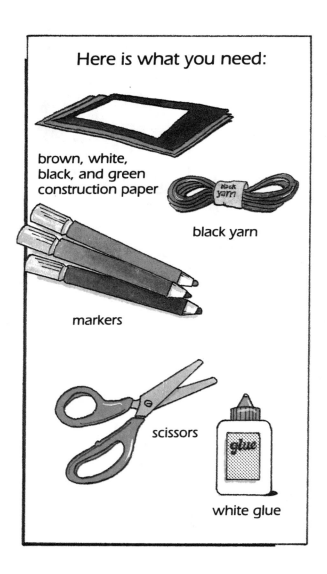

brown, white, black, and green construction paper

black yarn

markers

scissors

white glue

Here is what you do:

1. Cut a circle about the size of a dinner plate out of brown paper. Give the circle a face using paper cut-outs and markers. Glue on yarn hair.

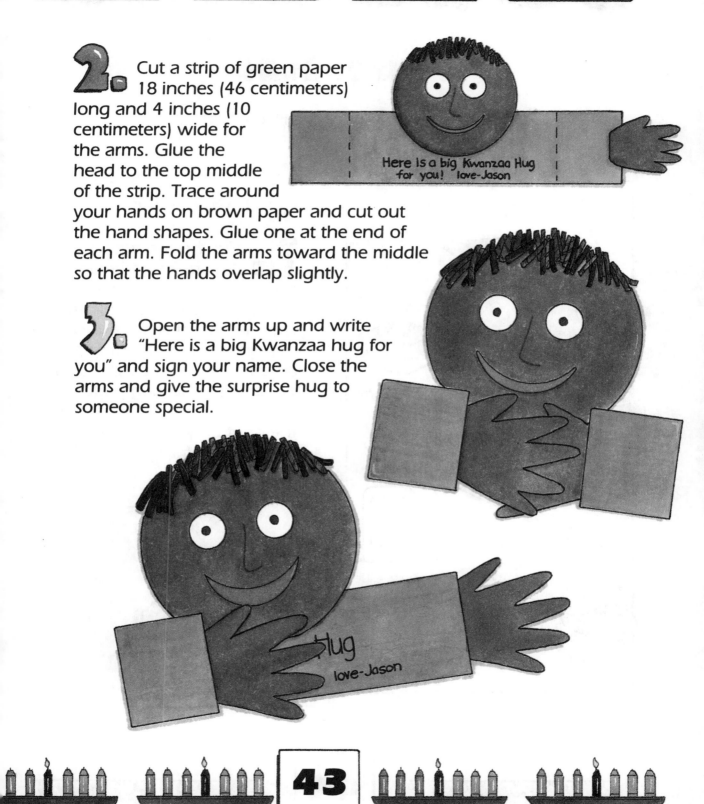

2. Cut a strip of green paper 18 inches (46 centimeters) long and 4 inches (10 centimeters) wide for the arms. Glue the head to the top middle of the strip. Trace around your hands on brown paper and cut out the hand shapes. Glue one at the end of each arm. Fold the arms toward the middle so that the hands overlap slightly.

3. Open the arms up and write "Here is a big Kwanzaa hug for you" and sign your name. Close the arms and give the surprise hug to someone special.

Here is a big Kwanzaa Hug for you! love-Jason

Hug love-Jason

Paper Hat

African men wear a hat called a **kufi**.

Here is what you need:

orange or tan construction paper, 12 by 18 inches (30 by 46 centimeters)

paper plate

an old sponge

three colors of poster paint

pencil

white glue

scissors

stapler

Here is what you do:

1. Cut the sponge into rectangles and triangles about 1 1/2 inches (4 centimeters) on each side. Dip the sponge shapes in various colors of paint, and use them to print an entire sheet of construction paper in a repeating pattern. Use your own ideas to design the print on your hat. Let the paper dry before you continue.

2. Position a paper plate toward one end of the printed paper, and trace around it. Cut the circle out. Cut two bands 3 1/2 inches (9 centimeters) wide from the other end and staple them together to fit your head. Place the band in the middle of the plain side of the circle and lightly trace around it with a pencil.

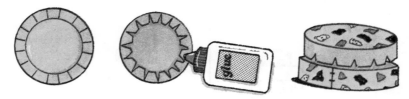

3. Cut slits 1 inch (2.5 centimeters) apart to form flaps all the way around the outside of the pencil circle. With the unprinted side of the paper up, fold all of the flaps in toward the center of the hat. Cover the outside (printed side) of the flaps with glue. Slide the circle down to the bottom of the band so that when you turn it over the print is on the outside of the hat.

Sand Beads

African women wear beautiful beads. Make some beads of your own to wear or give as a gift.

Here is what you need:

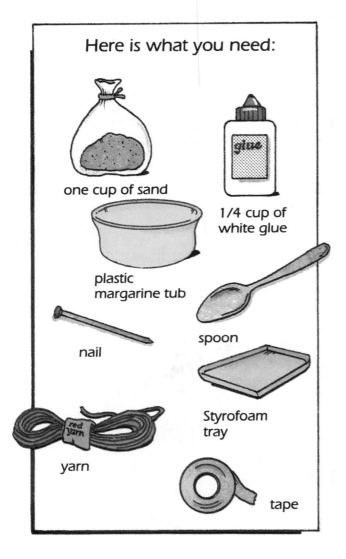

one cup of sand

1/4 cup of white glue

plastic margarine tub

nail

spoon

Styrofoam tray

yarn

tape

Here is what you do:

1. Mix the sand and glue in the plastic tub. Pinch off enough sand dough to roll a bead in the size you want. With the nail, poke a hole through the center for stringing. If the dough is too soft to hold the hole, add more sand until it is stiff enough so that the hole does not collapse.

2. Let the beads dry on a Styrofoam tray until hard. Make lots of beads.

3. Tape the end of a piece of yarn that is long enough to make a necklace, and string the beads on it. Tie the two ends together.

If you wish, you can decorate your beads before you string them by coloring them with markers or gluing tiny seed beads to them.

About the author and illustrator

Twenty years as a teacher and director of nursery school programs have given Kathy Ross extensive experience in guiding young children through craft projects. Her craft projects have appeared in **Highlights** magazine, and she has also written numerous songs for young children. She lives in Oneida, New York.

Sharon Lane Holm won awards for her work in advertising design before shifting her concentration to children's books. Her illustrations have since added zest to books for both the trade and educational markets. She lives in New Fairfield, Connecticut.